SO-EKZ-935

DATE DUE

523.2
KER
   Kerrod, Robin
    The solar system

MESA VERDE MIDDLE SCHOOL
8375 Entreken Way
San Diego, CA 92129

LET'S INVESTIGATE SCIENCE
SCIENCE
The Solar System

LET'S INVESTIGATE SCIENCE
The Solar System

Robin Kerrod

Illustrated by Ted Evans

MESA VERDE MIDDLE SCHOOL
8375 Entreken Way
San Diego, CA 92129

MARSHALL CAVENDISH
NEW YORK · LONDON · TORONTO · SYDNEY

Library Edition Published 1994

© Marshall Cavendish Corporation 1994

Published by Marshall Cavendish Corporation
2415 Jerusalem Avenue
PO Box 587
North Bellmore
New York 11710

Series created by Graham Beehag Book Design

All rights reserved. No part of this book may be reproduced or utilized in any form or by any means electronic or mechanical including photocopying, recording, or by any information storage and retrieval system, without permission from the copyright holders.

Library of Congress Cataloging-in-Publication Data

Kerrod, Robin.
    The solar sytem/ Robin Kerrod; llustrated by Ted Evans.
    p. cm. -- (Let's investigate science)
    Include index.
    Summary: Investigates the nature of the sun, the moon, the planets
    and other celestial bodies that make up our solar system.
    ISBN 1-85435-621-6 ISBN 1-85435-620-8 (set)
    1. Solar system -- Miscellanea -- Juvenile literature.
    [1. Solar system.] I. Evans, Ted ill. II. Title. III. Series: Kerrod,
    Robin. Let's investigate science.
    QB501.3.K58 1994   93-4339
    523.2--dc20   CIP
                                                  AC

MCC Editorial Consultant: Marvin Tolman, Ed.D.
                              Brigham Young University

Printed and bound in Hong Kong

Contents

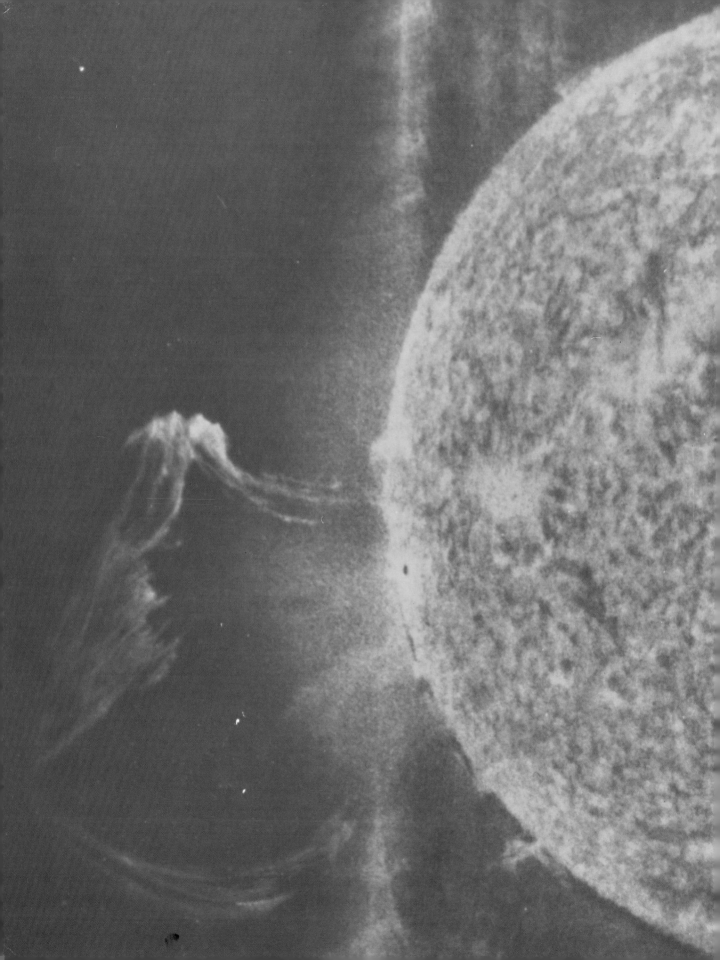

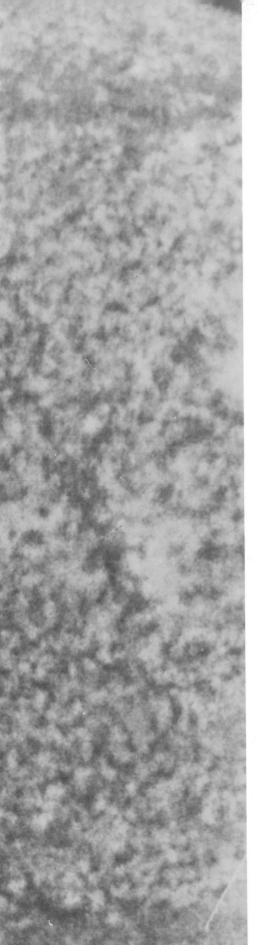

Introduction

The Earth, the planet we live on, hurtles through space along with a collection of other heavenly bodies, large and small. Together, they make up the Sun's family, or Solar System. The Solar System stretches over regions of space measured in billions upon billions of miles. Yet it occupies only a tiny part of a great Universe of stars, galaxies and space, which is bigger than we can ever imagine.

In this book we investigate the different bodies that make up the Solar System – the Sun, the Moon, the planets, their moons and a myriad of smaller bodies, such as asteroids and comets. We explore them from the Earth, with our eyes as well as with binoculars and telescopes. We also explore them at close quarters through the camera "eyes" of spacecraft, which have now journeyed to the farthest reaches of the Solar System.

You can check your answers to the questions featured throughout this book on pages 60-62.

◄ A huge fountain of red-hot gas leaps high above the surface of the Sun. The Sun lies at the heart of the Solar System, holding together a jumble of planets, asteroids, comets and other heavenly bodies.

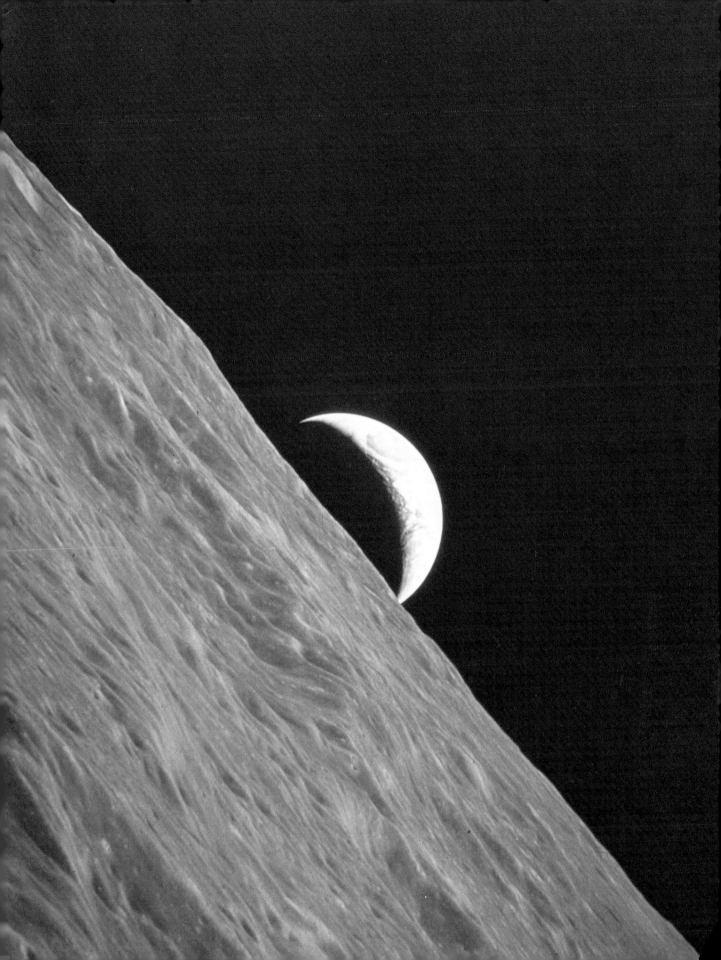

1 Sun, Earth and Moon

◄ The Earth appears in the dark Moon sky in this dramatic photograph taken by the Apollo astronauts. Neither the Moon nor the Earth shine by their own light. They are lit up by the distant Sun.

Locked together in the embrace of gravity, the Sun, the Earth and the Moon journey through space together. They are all different kinds of heavenly bodies. The Earth is a planet, the Moon is a satellite, and the Sun is a star.

The Sun is a huge globe of searing hot gas. It is similar to the other stars we see in the night sky. It appears much bigger and much brighter only because it is much closer.

At a distance of 93,000,000 miles (149,000,000 km), the Sun does not seem very close! But it is a stone's throw away compared with even the nearest stars.

Q **1.** The light from the Sun takes about 8½ minutes to reach us. The light from the nearest stars takes 4 YEARS to reach us! How far away are they?

▼ The Sun, the Earth and the Moon drawn to the same scale. The Sun could swallow a million Earths!

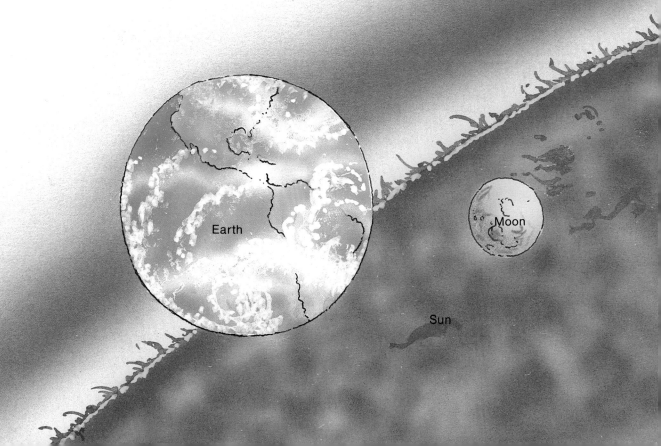

Earth

Moon

Sun

10

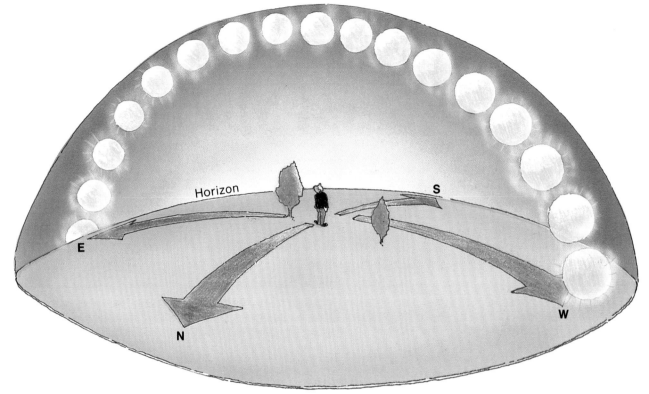

From the Earth, it looks as if the Sun is traveling from east to west across the sky (above). But in fact the Sun only appears to move. Really it is the Earth that is moving, spinning around on its axis (below).

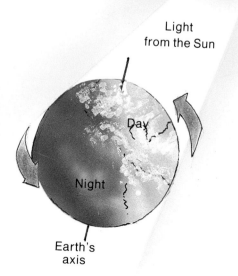

Sun

Light from the Sun

Day

Night

Earth's axis

Suntime

Early every morning, the Sun rises above the horizon in the east and brings light to our world. A new day dawns. The Sun appears to gradually move westward through the sky, climbing higher as it does so.

The Sun reaches its highest point at noon, and then in the afternoon gradually sinks lower until it dips below the horizon in the west. The sky darkens as the Sun sets, and night falls. It remains dark until the Sun rises again the next morning. Day and night make up the basic rhythm of nature occuring with the rising and setting of the Sun.

But the Sun does not actually move through the sky. It just appears to move. The reason it appears to travel toward the west is that the Earth is spinning in the opposite direction.

The Earth spins around in space on its axis like a top once every 24 hours. This period of time, a day, is our basic natural unit of time.

Q The Earth's diameter is 7,926 miles (12,756 km). How fast does a point on the Equator travel?

The yearly calendar

The Earth moves in space in another way. It travels in a circular path, or orbit, around the Sun, taking about 365 days to complete the journey. This period, a year, is the other main natural unit of time.

We base our calendar on a year of 365 days. And we split it up into 12 months, each of which has about four weeks of seven days each. The month is a period based loosely on the time it takes the Moon to go through its phases (see page 16). A week is roughly the time between one main phase and the next.

Q 2. The exact number of days in the natural year is 365 ¼. So our calendar year gets out of step with the natural year by one day every four years. How do we correct this?

11

The spinning Earth circles in orbit around the Sun. It makes one journey around the Sun in one year.

Q 1. The Earth lies 93,000,000 miles (149,000,000 km) from the Sun. How far does it travel in its orbit in a year?

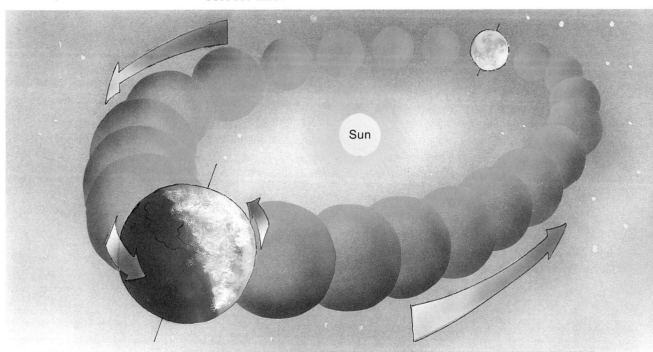

Sun

Star time

Our day of 24 hours is the time it takes the Earth to spin once on its axis, relative to the Sun.

But during this time, the Earth moves a little way along its orbit. And it has to spin around slightly more than one full circle to get back into the same position relative to the Sun.

This means that the Earth's actual time of spin, relative to the stars, is slightly under 24 hours. In fact, it is 23 hours 56 minutes. This period is the basis of sidereal time, or star time.

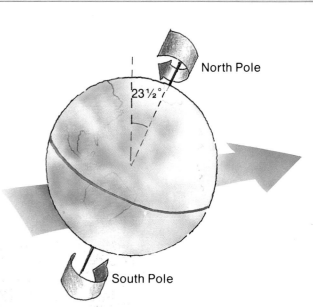

▲ **As the Earth circles around the Sun in space, its axis is slightly tilted in relation to the plane of its orbit. The imaginary points on the Earth's surface through which the axis passes are the North and South Poles.**

The changing seasons

Over much of the world, the temperature and weather vary with the seasons. Temperatures are lowest in the winter, start to rise in the spring, are highest in summer, start to drop in the autumn, and reach their lowest point again in the next winter.

These seasonal changes are caused by a tilt of the Earth's axis. The Earth does not spin upright, or on a perpendicular axis, as it travels around the Sun. Its axis is tilted 23 ½° from the perpendicular.

The axis always points in the same direction in space as the Earth circles the Sun. This means that during the year, the Earth's axis is tilted alternately toward, then away, from the Sun. And a place on the Earth's surface is slanted more toward the Sun at some times than at others.

In the Northern Hemisphere, a place slants the most toward the Sun on about June 21 each year. On this date the Sun climbs highest in the sky at noon, its rays are strongest, and the hours of daylight are longest. The temperature is high; it is the summer solstice.

On the other hand, a place slants the most away from the Sun on about December 21. On this date the Sun climbs to its lowest noontime position, its rays are weakest, and the daylight hours are shortest. The temperature is low; it is the winter solstice.

Equal days, equal nights

On two dates every year, the Earth's axis is tilted neither toward nor away from the Sun. This happens on about March 21 and September 23. On these dates, day and night are equally long all over the world. We call these dates the equinoxes ("equal nights"). March 21 is the spring, or vernal, equinox. It marks the beginning of spring in the Northern Hemisphere. September 23, the autumnal equinox, marks the beginning of autumn.

◀ At "America's Stonehenge" located near Salisbury, New Hampshire, the distant monolith ("single stone") forms part of one of the astronomical alignments at the site. Similar to Stonehenge in England, the alignments marked the different directions of the rising and setting Sun over the seasons in about 1500 BC.

▼ The Earth's axis keeps pointing in the same direction in space as the Earth circles the Sun. This brings about the four seasons of spring, summer, fall and winter.

Q 1. Why are the seasons opposite in the Northern and Southern Hemispheres?

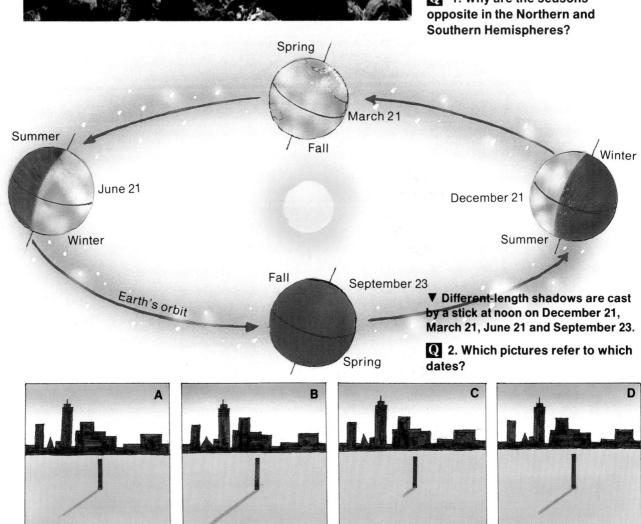

▼ Different-length shadows are cast by a stick at noon on December 21, March 21, June 21 and September 23.

Q 2. Which pictures refer to which dates?

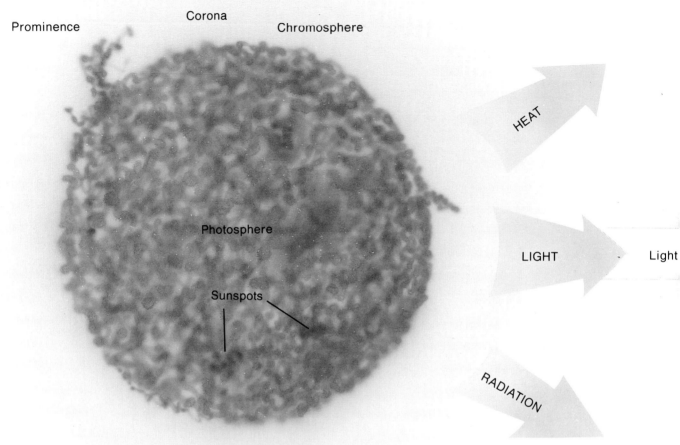

Prominence   Corona   Chromosphere

HEAT

LIGHT   Light

Photosphere

Sunspots

RADIATION

▲ The visible surface of the Sun is called the photosphere ("light-sphere"). Above is a pinkish layer of gas called the chromosphere ("color-sphere"). The corona ("crown") is the Sun's outer atmosphere.

WORKOUT

Every second the Sun loses over 4.4 million tons (4 million tonnes) of its mass in the nuclear processes that produce its energy. Figure out how much mass the Sun has lost while you have been alive.

The Sun

Our local star, the Sun, is a huge globe of searing hot, boiling gases. The main gas is hydrogen. With a diameter of about 865,000 miles (1,400,000 km), the Sun is more than 100 times the size of the Earth. Although the Sun lies 93,000,000 miles (149,000,000 km) away, it breathes life into our world. Without its heat and light, Earth would be cold, dark and lifeless.

The Sun has been shining for about 4.6 billion years and should continue to do so for at least as long again. How does it continue pouring out energy for so long?

It does so by means of nuclear reactions, which take place in the Sun's core, where temperatures reach 27,000,000°F (15,000,000°C). At such temperatures, hydrogen atoms combine, or fuse, together to form a different gas, named helium. During the process, called nuclear fusion, fantastic amounts of energy are given out as light, heat and other radiation.

The stormy Sun

The Sun is in continual turmoil. Great fountains of gas called prominences and tongues of flame called flares shoot high above the surface. Dark patches called sunspots come and go. They are about 3,600°F (2,000°C) cooler than the rest of the surface (about 11,000°F [6,000°C]).

These activities give rise to streams of particles that flow out into space and are called the solar wind.

The spectrum

Light is a kind of energy that travels in the form of a wave. But sunlight is a mixture of many waves. Each one has a different wavelength. What a prism does is separate out the various waves, which we then see as the different colors, the colors of the spectrum. These colors are the same ones we see in the rainbow.

Prism

▲ Sunlight is yellowish-white. But when you pass it through a prism, it splits up into a band of many colors we call the spectrum.

Q 1. Where can you see a spectrum in nature?

In order of increasing wavelength, the colors of the spectrum are violet, indigo, blue, green, yellow, orange and red.

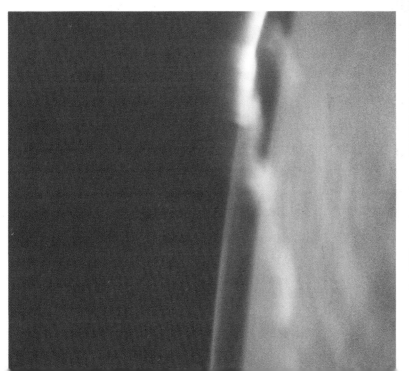

◄ A display of aurora, pictured from space. Auroras occur when particles in the solar wind react with air particles in the Earth's upper atmosphere.

Q 2. The popular name for the aurora in northern skies is the Northern . . . . . .

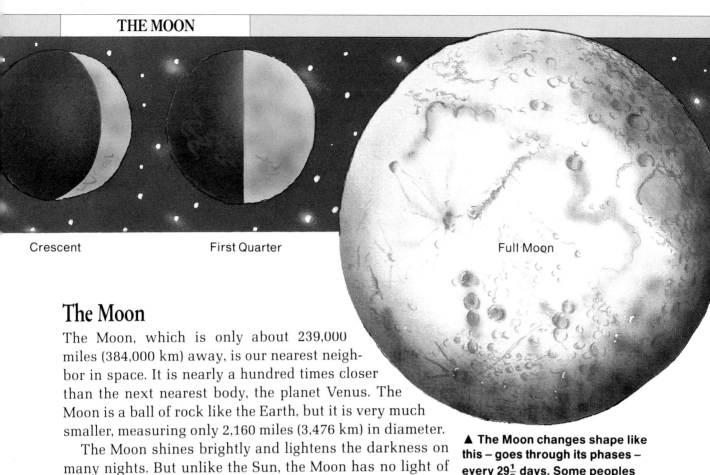

Crescent

First Quarter

Full Moon

The Moon

The Moon, which is only about 239,000 miles (384,000 km) away, is our nearest neighbor in space. It is nearly a hundred times closer than the next nearest body, the planet Venus. The Moon is a ball of rock like the Earth, but it is very much smaller, measuring only 2,160 miles (3,476 km) in diameter.

The Moon shines brightly and lightens the darkness on many nights. But unlike the Sun, the Moon has no light of its own. It shines beacause it reflects light from the Sun. As the Moon orbits around the Earth, we see dirrerent portions of it lit up, and the Moon appears to change shape. We call these changing shapes the Moon's phases.

▲ The Moon changes shape like this – goes through its phases – every 29½ days. Some peoples use this time period as the basis of their calendar year.

Q How far off is the lunar calendar from our usual one?

Match the phases

This diagram explains how the phases occur. The shape of the Moon we see depends on how far it has traveled in its orbit around the Earth.

The pictures at the top of the page show the different phases we see. The main phases are New, First Quarter, Full and Last Quarter. Look at the diagram and decide which positions (**A**, **M**, **H** and **Z**) correspond with the main phases shown above.

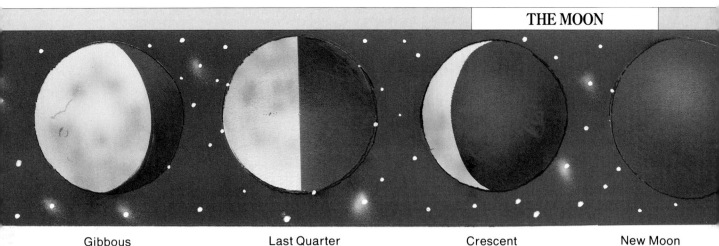

Gibbous   Last Quarter   Crescent   New Moon

INVESTIGATE

The Moon takes $27\frac{1}{3}$ days to travel once around the Earth. It also takes $27\frac{1}{3}$ days to spin around once on its axis. This has an important effect. Find out what it is by trying this:

Place a beachball on a table and imagine it is the Earth. Pretend your head is the Moon. Face the Earth. Now circle to your right a quarter of the way around the Earth, and at the same time spin around to the left a quarter of a turn. Repeat this three more times until you end up where you started. What do you find?

Weak gravity

Being so small, the Moon has a low mass, less than one-eightieth of the mass of the Earth. Because of its low mass, its gravity is low, just one-sixth that of the Earth.

With its low gravity, the Moon has been unable to hold back any gases to make an atmosphere. So there is no air to support colorful plants and animals. There is also no water. The Moon is an airless, colorless, dead, dry and silent world. (Quick . . .why is it silent?)

Even though the Moon's gravity is low, it still affects us on Earth. When it is overhead, it tugs at the waters in the oceans, causing them to rise, as a high tide.

Q The Moon is overhead at any place only once a day, as the Earth spins around once. So why do we get two high tides a day?

The Moon's surface

The Moon is so close to us that we can see details on its surface even with the naked eye. We can see that it is divided into light and dark areas. Thinking the Moon might be another world like the Earth, early astronomers thought the light areas might be land and the dark areas seas. They called the dark areas "maria" (singular "mare"), the Latin word for seas.

18

We still use the terms "seas" and "mare" today, even though we know that they are in reality vast, dusty plains.

Q **1.** Why can't the Moon have seas like the Earth?

▲ Craters pepper much of the Moon's surface. This is Eratosthenes, easy to spot because it is surrounded by a low-lying sea.

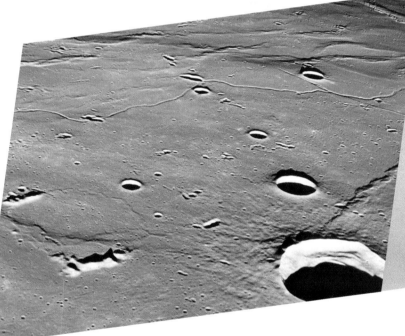

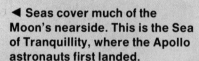

◄ Seas cover much of the Moon's nearside. This is the Sea of Tranquillity, where the Apollo astronauts first landed.

▼ Highlands present some of the most dramatic landscapes on the Moon. This is a highland region around the crater Tycho.

Cratered highlands

The light areas on the Moon turn out to be highlands. They contrast markedly with the seas. Whereas the seas are relatively flat and smooth, the highlands are mountainous and rugged. They are almost completely covered with large and small craters. The craters were formed when meteorites bombarded the Moon ages ago.

Q **2.** The Earth was also bombarded then. Why aren't there still a lot of craters on Earth?

Close-ups

Through powerful binoculars or a small telescope, the Moon is a magnificent sight. Literally hundreds of craters swim into view. At the time of the Full Moon, look out for the craters Copernicus and Tycho. They are surrounded by brilliant rays.

Q 2. Look at the Moon first through binoculars, then through a telescope. Do you notice any difference?

▼ The Full Moon as we see it from Earth, showing the most prominent seas and craters.

Q 1. The dark seas and the lighter highland areas are of different ages. Which do you think are the oldest, seas or highlands? Give your reasons.

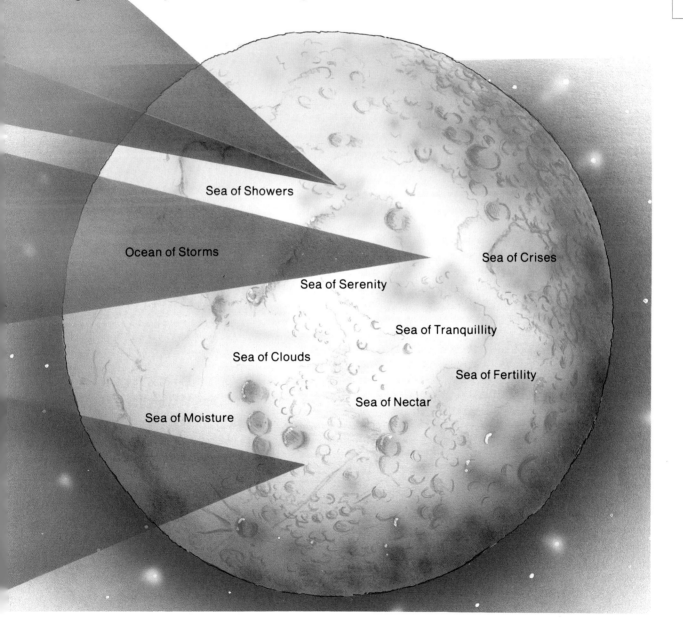

Sea of Showers

Ocean of Storms

Sea of Crises

Sea of Serenity

Sea of Tranquillity

Sea of Clouds

Sea of Fertility

Sea of Nectar

Sea of Moisture

Man on the Moon

On July 20, 1969, a curious spacecraft, looking a little like a spider, touched down on the Moon's Sea of Tranquillity. A few hours later its hatch opened, and down stepped the first human being to set foot on another world.

He was the Apollo 11 astronaut Neil Armstrong. Over the next three-and-a-half years, eleven more astronauts followed in his footsteps. They explored six different regions of the Moon, lowlands, highlands and valleys. Altogether they collected 847 lb (385 kg) of Moon rock and soil, and took thousands of stunning photographs that still amaze us even today.

20

Apollo spacecraft

The astronauts who roamed over the Moon traveled there in the Apollo spacecraft. This was a three-part craft, which carried a crew of three. They traveled for the most part in the CSM (command and service modules). The third part was the lunar module (LEM), which carried the two moon-walkers down to the Moon and back.

Q **1.** When the LEM left the Earth, it weighed 33,000 lb (15,000 kg). On the Moon it weighed only 5,500 lb (2,500 kg). What happened to the other 27,500 lb (12,500 kg)?

IT'S AMAZING!

The rocket that launched the Apollo spacecraft to the Moon was the biggest rocket ever. On the launch pad it stood no less than 365 feet (111 meters) tall. It weighed nearly 3,300 tons (3,000 tonnes), and had the power of a whole fleet of jumbo jets!

◄This is one of the most famous of all space photographs. It shows the second man to walk on the Moon, during the Apollo 11 mission. His name is Edwin Aldrin. The photographer, reflected in Aldrin's helmet, is the first man on the Moon, Neil Armstrong.

Q **2. Why did the Apollo astronauts have to wear spacesuits on the Moon?**

▲ Apollo 16 astronaut Charles Duke takes the lunar rover for a spin on the Moon. This "Moon buggy" had a top speed of about 10 mph (15 km/h) and was powered by electric motors.

Q 1. Why couldn't it be driven by an ordinary car's gasoline engine?

The scientific harvest

The Apollo astronauts spent a total of 170 hours exploring the Moon. They not only collected rocks, but also drilled into the rocks to take "core samples" that revealed the Moon's past history. They also set up scientific stations at each landing site. The instruments included seismometers, which measured ground tremors, or "moonquakes."

Study of the Moon rocks shows that these are mainly two different types. One is like the dark volcanic rock called basalt found on Earth. Another is like the Earth rock breccia, which is made up of cemented rock chips. All the Moon rocks are much older than the rocks on the Earth's surface, up to 4 billion years old.

Q 2. Mostly, the minerals in the Moon rocks were found to be similar to those found in Earth rocks. But one mineral was quite different. Scientists named it armalcolite. Can you figure out why?

WARNING
NEVER look directly at the Sun, even during a total eclipse.

Shadows in space

It is a strange coincidence that the Sun and the Moon appear about the same size in the sky. And in its orbit around the Earth, the Moon sometimes passes in front of the Sun during the day and casts a shadow on the Earth. We call such an event an eclipse of the Sun, or a solar eclipse.

If the Moon only partly covers the Sun, a partial eclipse occurs. Sunlight fades a little. But when the Moon completely covers the Sun, a total eclipse occurs. Day turns suddenly into night. If we look at the Moon, we see little pinkish points around the edges. These are solar prominences, fountains of gas. We also see a white halo, which is the corona, the Sun's outer atmosphere. But totality, or total darkness, lasts for only a few minutes at most.

The Earth also casts a shadow in space, and sometimes the Moon passes into it. We call this an eclipse of the Moon, or a lunar eclipse. Lunar eclipses last much longer than solar eclipses.

Q 1. Why is this?

WORKOUT

The Sun measures about 865,000 miles (1,392,000 km) across and is about 93,000,000 miles (149,000,000 km) from Earth. The Moon measures about 2,160 miles (3,476 km) across and at times lies about 231,500 miles (372,500 km) away.

Figure out how many times bigger the Sun is than the Moon, and how many times farther away it is. How does this explain why total solar eclipses occur?

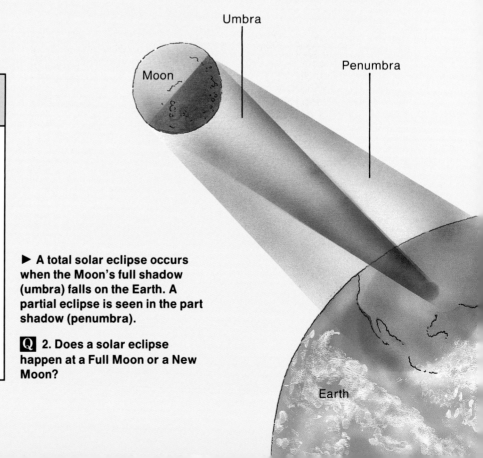

► A total solar eclipse occurs when the Moon's full shadow (umbra) falls on the Earth. A partial eclipse is seen in the part shadow (penumbra).

Q 2. Does a solar eclipse happen at a Full Moon or a New Moon?

◀ Total solar eclipse, Hawaii, July 1991: Here the Moon has already taken a huge bite out of the Sun.

Sun

Earth

Earth's shadow

Moon

▲ During totality, the Sun's brilliant pearly white corona is visible around the dark disc of the Moon.

WORKOUT

At the distance of the Moon, the Earth's shadow measures about 5,700 miles (9,170 km) across. The Moon measures 2,160 miles (3,476 km) across and moves at a speed of about 2,260 mph (3,630 km/h). Work out how long the Moon is in total eclipse using these numbers.

▲ A total lunar eclipse occurs when the Moon passes into the Earth's shadow in space.

Q Does a lunar eclipse happen at a Full Moon or a New Moon?

2
The Sun's Family

25

◀ The planet Saturn, often called the "jewel of the Solar System." It is a beautiful object when seen through a telescope because of the shining rings that circle its equator. This picture was taken by a Voyager probe.

▼ The planets travel within a certain band of sky, which we call the zodiac. They travel through 12 constellations, called the constellations of the zodiac.

The Earth and the Moon travel through space with the Sun and a host of other bodies, which together make up the Solar System. The Sun's "family" also includes eight more planets, over 60 more moons, together with tens of thousands of smaller bodies. These include mini-planets called asteroids, icy comets and tiny bits of rock that rain down on the Earth as meteors.

This extended family of the Sun is scattered over distances measured in millions and billions of miles. It is kept together by the immense pull of the Sun's gravity. But mostly the Solar System is empty space.

All the planets circle the Sun in the same direction and in much the same plane (flat sheet). That is why we may see them traveling in a somewhat narrow band against the background of stars.

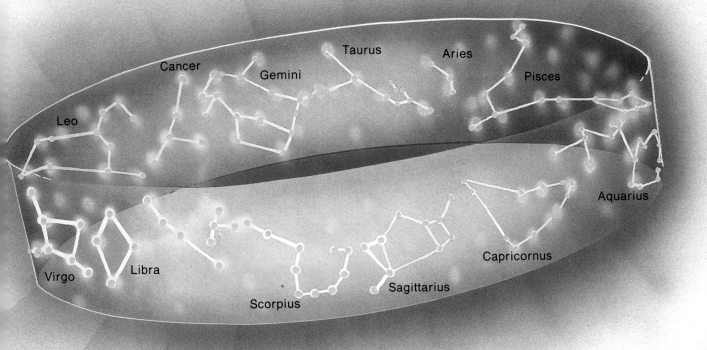

Cancer · Taurus · Aries · Gemini · Pisces · Leo · Virgo · Libra · Scorpius · Sagittarius · Capricornus · Aquarius

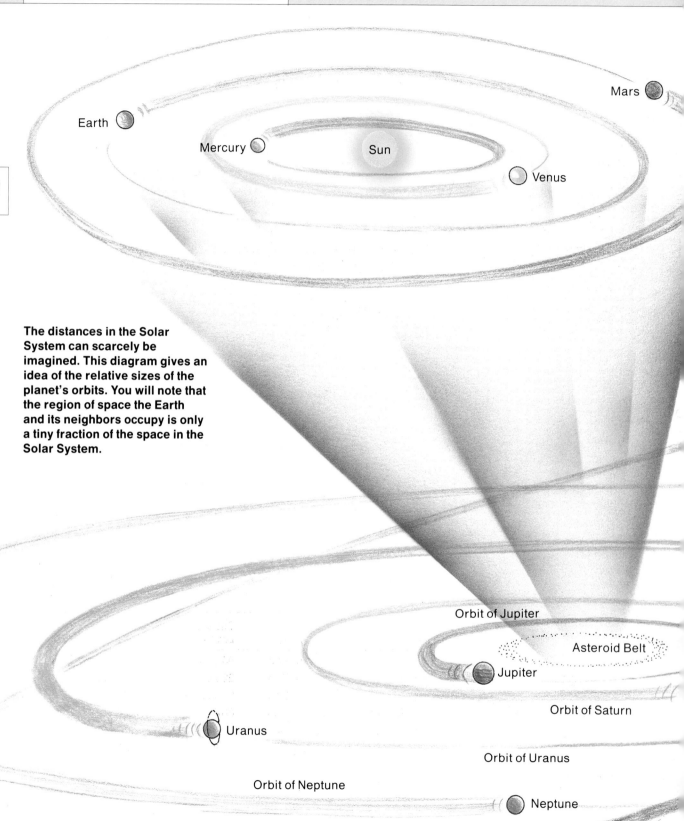

Earth

Mercury

Sun

Venus

Mars

The distances in the Solar System can scarcely be imagined. This diagram gives an idea of the relative sizes of the planet's orbits. You will note that the region of space the Earth and its neighbors occupy is only a tiny fraction of the space in the Solar System.

Orbit of Jupiter

Asteroid Belt

Jupiter

Orbit of Saturn

Uranus

Orbit of Uranus

Orbit of Neptune

Neptune

INVESTIGATE

The average distance from the Earth to the Sun is 93,000,000 miles (149,000,000 km). Astronomers call this one astronomical unit (AU). Using the figures in the Table below, figure out the distances of the planets from the Sun in astronomical units.

Sizing up the Solar System

The Earth circles in space around the Sun at a distance of some 93,000,000 miles (149,000,000 km). Two planets circle closer in, Mercury and Venus, and the other six planets circle farther out. In order of increasing distance, they are Mars, Jupiter, Saturn, Uranus, Neptune and Pluto.

The inner four planets lie relatively close together. Beyond Mars, the distance between the planets begins to widen dramatically, as the diagram shows.

If you could look down on the Earth from "north" of the Solar System, you would find that it circles the Sun in a counterclockwise direction. All the other planets also circle in this direction.

Years and days

The time it takes a planet to circle once around the Sun (which we can call its "year") depends on its speed and how far out it is. The Earth takes about 365 days to circle once, but Pluto takes nearly 250 Earth-years.

The Earth spins on its axis every 24 hours, giving us our "day." The other planets spin on their axes, too. With the exception of Mars, their "days" are much shorter or longer than the Earth's.

Orbit of Pluto

Pluto

Saturn

Planet	Distance from Sun (miles)	Time taken to circle Sun	Spins on axis in
Mercury	36 million	88 days	59 days
Venus	67 million	225 days	243 days
Earth	93 million	365.25 days	23 hrs 56 mins
Mars	142 million	687 days	24 hrs 37 mins
Jupiter	483 million	11.9 years	9 hrs 55 mins
Saturn	887 million	29.5 years	10 hrs 12 mins
Uranus	1,783 million	84 years	16 hrs 19 mins
Neptune	2,794 million	165 years	16 hrs
Pluto	3,666 million	248 years	6 days 8 hrs

Sizing up the planets

The Earth is the biggest of the four planets in the inner part of the Solar System. It is slightly bigger than Venus and much bigger than Mars and Mercury.

All these planets are made up mainly of rock. They have a hard "crust" on the surface, a softer rocky "mantle" underneath, and a partly molten "core" at the center. The core is made up mainly of the metals iron and nickel.

The planets are relatively heavy; that is, they have a relatively high density, about five times the density of water. Nevertheless, the Earth weighs more than the other three planets put together.

28

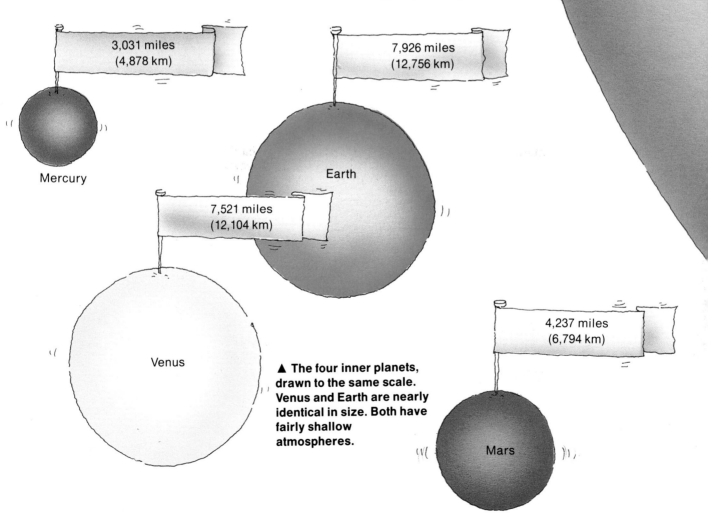

88,700 miles
(142,800 km)

Jupiter

▶ Segments representing the size of the giant outer planets, drawn to the same scale as the inner ones. All four planets have very deep atmospheres.

3,031 miles
(4,878 km)

Mercury

7,926 miles
(12,756 km)

Earth

7,521 miles
(12,104 km)

Venus

▲ The four inner planets, drawn to the same scale. Venus and Earth are nearly identical in size. Both have fairly shallow atmospheres.

4,237 miles
(6,794 km)

Mars

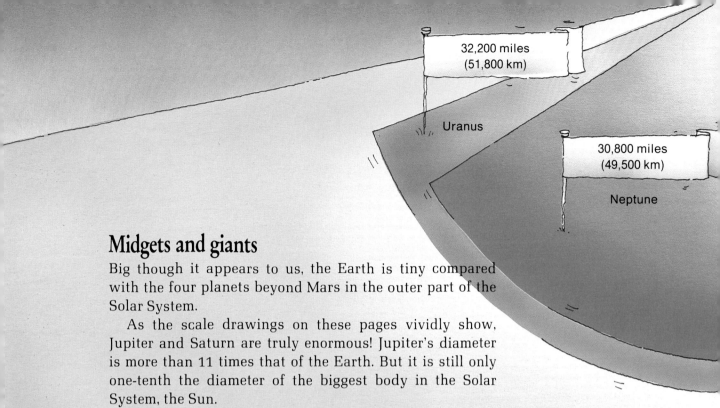

32,200 miles
(51,800 km)

Uranus

30,800 miles
(49,500 km)

Neptune

Midgets and giants

Big though it appears to us, the Earth is tiny compared with the four planets beyond Mars in the outer part of the Solar System.

As the scale drawings on these pages vividly show, Jupiter and Saturn are truly enormous! Jupiter's diameter is more than 11 times that of the Earth. But it is still only one-tenth the diameter of the biggest body in the Solar System, the Sun.

Like the Sun, Jupiter and the other giants are made up mainly of gas. They are relatively light for their size.

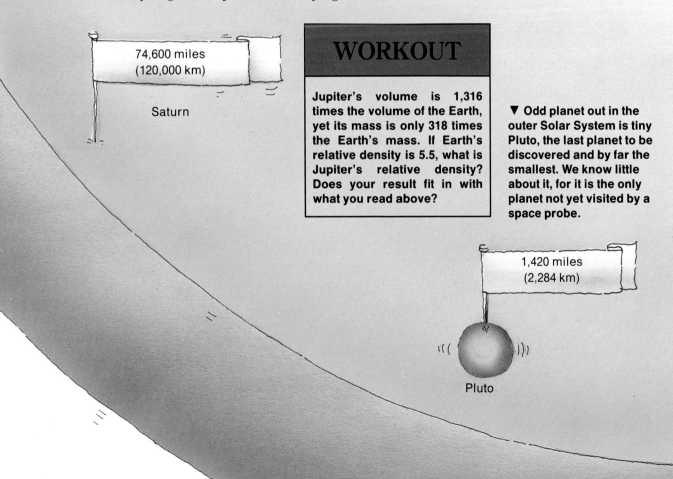

74,600 miles
(120,000 km)

Saturn

WORKOUT

Jupiter's volume is 1,316 times the volume of the Earth, yet its mass is only 318 times the Earth's mass. If Earth's relative density is 5.5, what is Jupiter's relative density? Does your result fit in with what you read above?

▼ Odd planet out in the outer Solar System is tiny Pluto, the last planet to be discovered and by far the smallest. We know little about it, for it is the only planet not yet visited by a space probe.

1,420 miles
(2,284 km)

Pluto

Spotting the planets

In the night sky we, like our ancestors before us, can see five planets with the naked eye. They are Mercury, Venus, Mars, Jupiter and Saturn. They look like bright stars.

But how can we tell the difference between the planets and bright stars? That is quite simple. The bright stars always stay in the same relative positions in the heavens, and the planets appear to wander about.

The stars are "fixed" within their constellations, or star patterns. They do not appear to change even after centuries. The planets, however, move through the constellations month by month. In fact, the word "planet" means "wandering star."

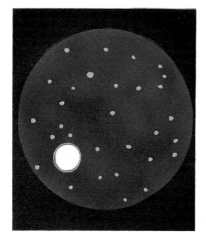

▲ Viewed through binoculars, the planets show a distinct disc. The stars remain as pinpoints of light.

▼ The path of Mars through the heavens between July and November 1992. It passed through the constellations Taurus and Gemini.

INVESTIGATE

Plotting the planets
Try plotting the path of the planets yourself. Mars and Jupiter are the best ones to choose. Plot their positions among the constellations every few days. Astronomy magazines and some newspapers carry charts to help you locate them.

Q Why are Mars and Jupiter the best planets to choose? (Read "Exploring the planets," beginning on page 38.)

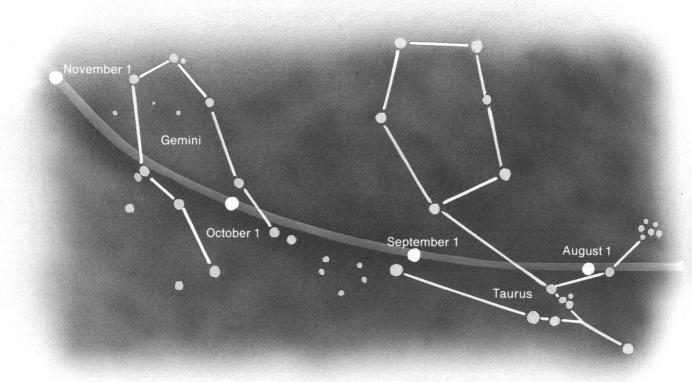

November 1

Gemini

October 1

September 1

August 1

Taurus

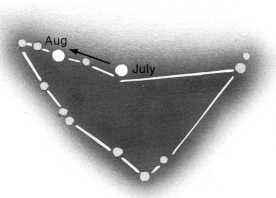

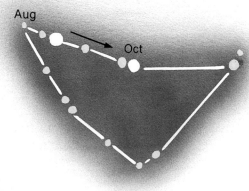

◄ For much of 1992 the planet Saturn stayed within the constellation Capricornus. Between July and August it traveled a short distance in the usual direction, that is, toward the east (to the left).

► Between August and October, however, Saturn doubled back on itself, traveling toward the west (to the right). By November, it was traveling eastward once more.

◄ This was the kind of path Saturn took through the heavens in 1992. We find that Mars and Jupiter also show such backward, or retrograde, motion at times.

The zodiac

The planets can always be found within a narrow band of the sky called the zodiac. The constellations they travel through are Aries, Pisces, Aquarius, Capricornus, Sagittarius, Scorpius, Libra, Virgo, Leo, Cancer, Gemini and Taurus.

The 12 constellations of the zodiac are important in astrology. Astrologers believe that the movements and positions of the planets among the stars can affect human lives. But there is no scientific evidence for this.

Q Find out under which star sign you were born. Do you have anything in common with other people born under the same sign?

◀ This glowing cloud of gas is known as the Orion nebula. It is in such clouds that stars and solar systems are born.

Q 1. Where in the sky can you see the Orion nebula? Why is it special?

▲ Nearly 5 billion years ago the matter that became our Solar System might have looked like this. In the center was a globe-shaped mass that was getting hotter and hotter. Other matter formed a disc around it, spinning rapidly.

Q 2. What other heavenly bodies have this shape?

Birth of the Solar System

The Solar System is very old. Astronomers think it was born about 4.6 billion years ago. At that time, the corner of space the Solar System now occupies was sprinkled with gas and dust. The gas and dust formed a very thin cloud in space, a cloud we call a nebula.

For some reason, the cloud started to collapse. The gas and dust particles began to come together under gravity to form a denser and denser mass, which started to rotate. The more it collapsed, the faster it rotated. Over time it formed into a disc, with a bulge in the middle.

As it shrank more and more, the bulge became globe-shaped and became hotter and hotter. Eventually, it became so hot that it started to shine as a star, a star we call the Sun. Meanwhile, matter in the disc was clumping together into bigger and bigger lumps. These lumps became the planets and their moons.

Sorting the planets

The matter in the inner part of the disc was hotter than that in the outer part. This temperature difference probably explains the difference in make-up between the mainly solid inner planets and the mainly gaseous outer planets.

Gas in the inner, hotter parts of the disc was driven off, leaving just solid material. But gas remained in the cooler, outer parts and built up around the bodies forming there.

Leftovers

During the formation of the planets and their moons, many rocky bits were left over. Thousands of them, the asteroids, circle the Sun between the orbits of Mars and Jupiter. Many other bits of rock, ice and dust drift far beyond the planets at the very edge of the Solar System. We see some of them as comets when they stray in toward the Sun.

▼ This rocky lump is the tiny Martian moon Phobos, only about 18 miles (30 km) across. It is probably a captured asteroid.

▲ In time the particles in the spinning disc began colliding with one another and sticking together to form larger and larger lumps. The lumps attracted one another to form bigger and bigger bodies until they became the size of the planets as we know them today.

Ⓠ 3. Why were the lumps attracted to one another?

Comets

Comets are among the most spectacular of all the heavenly bodies. They can appear without warning and appear to grow from a pinprick of light to a blazing torch that out-shines the brightest planets. They can grow a tail that may stretch for hundreds of millions of miles across the sky.

What are comets? They are lumps of rock, dust and ice, a lot like large "dirty snowballs." Most measure just a few dozen miles across.

Comets spend most of their time in the depths of the Solar System. There they stay frozen and invisible. Only when they travel in toward the Sun do they begin to shine.

Heads and tails

As a comet draws closer to the Sun, the heat of the Sun starts to melt the ice and turn it to gas. The gas and the dust are released and form a cloud that reflects sunlight, and the comet becomes visible. It grows in size and brightness as more and more gas and dust are released from its core, or nucleus. The solar wind (see page 15) often "blows" away the dust to give the comet a tail.

After the comet loops around the Sun, it begins its journey back to the depths of the Solar System. It gradually appears smaller and dimmer, and loses its tail as it cools down and freezes. Eventually, it disappears from view.

▼ A comet becomes visible in the night sky and grows a tail when it approaches the Sun.

Q What do you notice about the comet's orbit? Its tail?

Orbit of comet

Sun

▲ This photograph of Halley's comet was taken in 1986. It is a time exposure, in which the camera followed the comet for several minutes. The streaks are trails made by the background stars.

Q 1. Why aren't the stars just points of light?

Happy returns

Most comets follow open, curved paths through the Solar System and may not return to view in Earth's skies for thousands of years, if ever. But some comets appear at regular and more frequent intervals. They follow closed, elliptical orbits and stay within or close to the orbits of the planets.

We call these regular visitors periodic comets. The best known is Halley's comet, which appears every 75-76 years. It is named after the English astronomer who first realized it is a regular visitor.

Doomsday comets

Ancient peoples were terrified when comets suddenly appeared in the sky. They thought that comets were evil and would bring bad luck, famine and disaster.

A comet may have been responsible for the deaths of the dinosaurs and other types of animals 65 million years ago. It is thought that a comet 6-12 miles (10-20 km) across slammed into the Earth, sending enormous amounts of dust into the atmosphere. The dust stayed there for months, totally blotting out the Sun.

Q 2. Why would this have caused the dinosaurs to die out?

◀ Europe's space probe Giotto sent back this picture of the heart of Halley's comet in March 1986. It is a potato-shaped lump of rock about 10 miles (15 km) across.

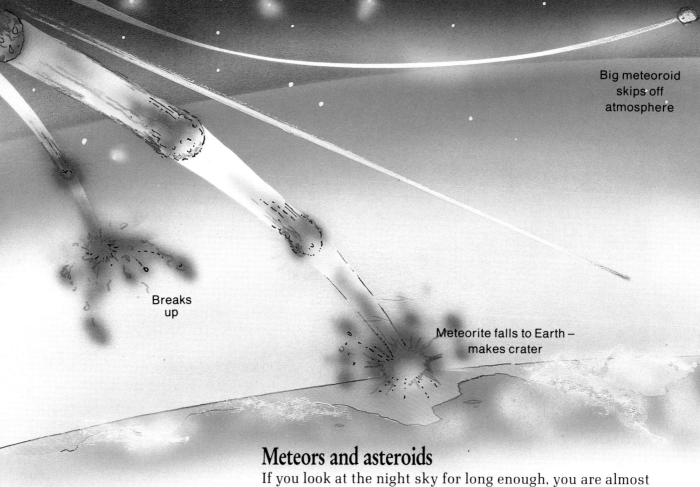

Big meteoroid
skips off
atmosphere

Breaks
up

Meteorite falls to Earth –
makes crater

Small bits of rock from outer space burn up completely when they enter the atmosphere. Large pieces may survive to reach the ground as meteorites. Others may "bounce" off the atmosphere and disappear back into space.

IT'S AMAZING!

The mass of the Earth increases by more than 5 million tons (4.5 million tonnes) a year because of the dust it receives from burned-up meteorites.

Meteors and asteroids

If you look at the night sky for long enough, you are almost certain to see a shooting star. This is the popular name for a meteor. A meteor is a fiery trail left behind when a speck of rock burns up in the air.

On most nights you should be able to see two or three meteors every hour. But at times you could see as many as 50! This would happen during a meteor "shower." One of the best showers, the Perseid, takes place in August each year.

Space is full of bits of rock, called meteoroids. When they come near the Earth, they are attracted to it by gravity. They plunge into the atmosphere at speeds as high as 40 miles (70 km) a second. Friction with the air produces enough heat to set them alight.

Most meteoroids are not much bigger than grains of sand, and they burn up completely. A few are much bigger and travel down to the ground, as meteorites. If they are big enough, they may hit the ground with such force that they dig out huge craters, like the Arizona Meteor Crater.

Some meteorites are stony and are made up mainly of rock. Others are metallic and are made up mainly of a mixture of nickel and iron.

◄ The famous Meteor Crater in Arizona. It was made by a huge meteorite about 50,000 years ago. It measures about 4,150 feet (1,265 meters) across and is about 575 feet (175 meters) deep.

WORKOUT

The amount of rock gouged out when the Arizona meteorite struck was colossal. Figure out roughly how much in tons (tonnes). Assume the crater is a disc 4,150 feet (1,265 meters) in diameter and 574 feet (175 meters) thick, and the density of the rock is 3 tons per cubic yard (3.5 tonnes per cubic meter).

The starlike asteroids

Between the orbits of Mars and Jupiter, there is quite a gap where we might expect to find another planet. But when we view this gap through a telescope, we can see not one fairly big planet, but thousands of tiny ones. Even the biggest, named Ceres, is only about 620 miles (1,000 km) across.

We call these tiny "planets" asteroids, or minor planets. Most of them orbit the Sun in a broad band called the asteroid belt. A few "Earth-grazers" have orbits that take them uncomfortably close to Earth.

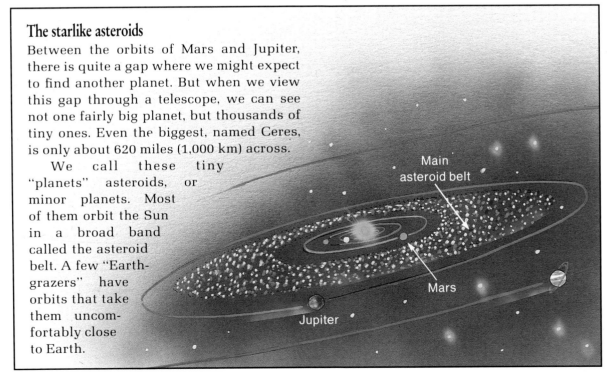

Main asteroid belt

Mars

Jupiter

3
Exploring the Planets

◄ **The giant planet Jupiter (top) and the four largest of its moons, pictured in a montage of Voyager photos. The moon at top left is Io; then, going down the page, come Europa and Ganymede. At bottom right is part of Callisto. All these moons can be seen through binoculars.**

▼ **Reminder: This is the order of the planets as you travel outward from the Sun. The diagram is not drawn to scale. (Pluto sometimes travels within Neptune's orbit (see page 26-27).**

The nine planets that circle the Sun are all quite different from one another. They differ not only in size, but also in appearance and what they are made of.

The planets closest to Earth – Mercury, Venus and Mars – are most like the Earth in that they are made up of rock. They are often called the terrestrial (Earthlike) planets. But they are quite unlike the Earth in one respect: they have no life on them.

Nor is life found on the more distant planets, Jupiter, Saturn, Uranus, Neptune and Pluto. Except for Pluto, all these planets are giants compared with the Earth. They are huge and they have very deep atmospheres of gas, with only a tiny rocky center. We know such things about these distant giants because robotic spacecraft such as Pioneer 10 and 11 and Voyager 1 and 2 have visited them and reported back what they found.

Sun　Mercury　Venus　Earth　Mars　Jupiter　Saturn　Uranus　Neptune　Pluto

Mercury and Venus

These two planets are both closer to the Sun than the Earth is, and they therefore stay near the Sun in the sky. For this reason, they can be seen only just before the Sun rises, or just after it has set. Before sunrise, they are called morning stars, and after sunset, evening stars. Jupiter and Mars also on occasion shine in the morning or evening sky. Jupiter can be confused with Venus because of its bright white light, but Mars can be readily identified by its reddish color.

Mercury is often difficult to see because it never rises far above the horizon while the sky is dark. And it is never very bright because it is very small. It is the second smallest planet, only 3,031 miles (4,878 km) across. Being so small, it does not have enough gravity to be able to hold on to any atmosphere.

Because it is close to the Sun, Mercury gets very hot, reaching temperatures of 800°F (430°C) or more. This is hot enough to melt lead!

40

▼ Mercury and Venus both circle inside the Earth's orbit.

Q 1. At which point or points in their orbits can we see them best, A, B, C or D?

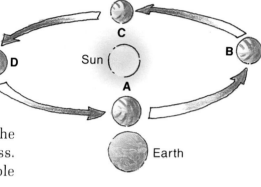

▼ This diagram shows the path of Mercury at a time when it is following the Sun across the sky, and Venus at a time when it is preceding the Sun across the sky.

Q 2. On these occasions, which planet would be a morning star? An evening star?

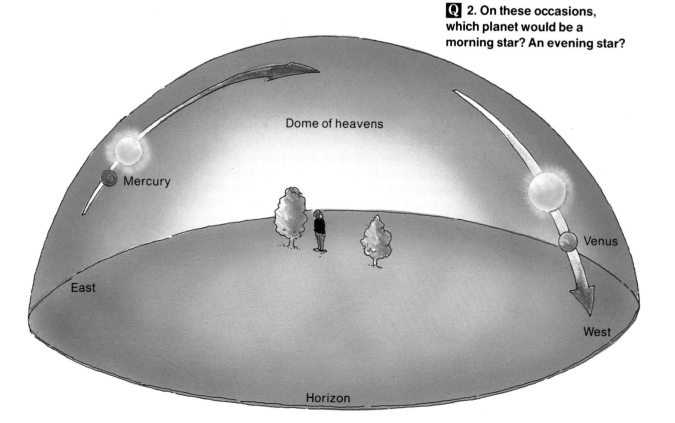

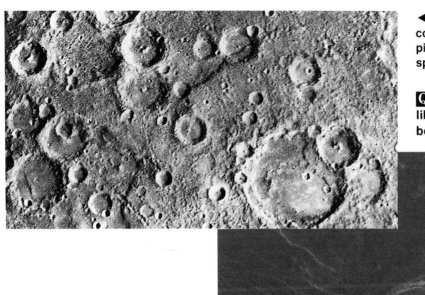

◄ The surface of Mercury is covered with craters, as this picture taken by the Mariner 10 space probe shows.

Q Mercury looks very much like another familiar heavenly body. Which one?

▶ Not many craters scar the surface of Venus. Radar pictures like this, taken by the Magellan probe, have shown the planet to have rolling plains and highland areas.

Hostile Venus

Although it is farther away from the Sun, Venus is even hotter than Mercury! This is because its thick atmosphere acts like a greenhouse and traps the Sun's heat. Its surface temperature can reach 900°F (480°C).

The atmosphere consists mainly of carbon dioxide at nearly 100 times the atmospheric pressure on Earth. It is filled with white clouds, which are so dense that we cannot see through them. The only way we can "see" through the clouds is by radar.

Venus, which is a near-twin of the Earth in size, is also the planet that comes closest to us. At times it comes within 26,000,000 miles (42,000,000 km). For this reason it shines brilliantly in the sky as either a morning or evening star. No other heavenly body, except for the Sun and the Moon, shines so brightly.

IT'S AMAZING!

On some nights when Venus shines at its brightest, you can see your own shadow.

Three things set Earth apart
from the other planets: an
abundance of air, water and life.

Q Why are the first two vital
for the third?

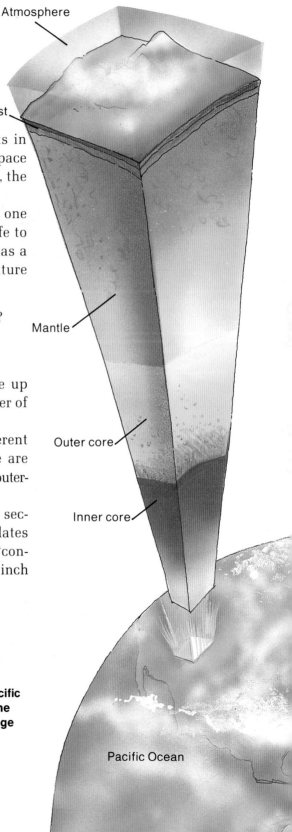

▶ If you could cut a wedge from the Earth, this is what you might find. The crust averages about 18 miles (30 km) thick, the mantle about 1,800 miles (2,900 km) thick, and the outer core about 1,150 miles (1,850 km) thick.

Q 1. What is the diameter of the inner core?

Atmosphere

Crust

Mantle

Outer core

Inner core

Planet Earth

Our home, the Earth, is like most of the other planets in some respects. It spins on its axis as it circles in space around the Sun, and it has a satellite circling around it, the Moon.

But the Earth differs from all the other planets in one vital respect. On Earth, conditions are just right for life to occur. On other planets they are not. Only the Earth has a breathable atmosphere, plenty of water, and a temperature that is not too hot or too cold.

Q 2. Which gas in the atmosphere is essential for life?

A crusty Earth

Like its three planetary neighbors, the Earth is made up mainly of rock. It is bigger than they are, with a diameter of 7,926 miles (12,756 km) at the Equator.

Our planet is made up of a number of layers of different composition. The hard outer crust and softer mantle are made up of rock; the core is made up of nickel and iron. The outerpart is liquid.

The soft mantle is moving slowly, carrying with it sections, or "plates," of the crust. The movement of the plates is causing the continents to move slowly apart. Such "continental drift" is making the Atlantic Ocean about 1 inch (2.5 cm) wider every year.

▶ Great oceans like the Pacific cover about 70 per cent of the Earth's surface. They average over 2.5 miles (4 km) deep.

Pacific Ocean

Mars

Mars is one of the easiest planets to spot in the night sky. At its brightest, it outshines all the other planets except Venus. But the main thing that makes it easy to spot is its color, which is reddish-orange. By contrast, Venus and the other really bright planet, Jupiter, are brilliant white.

Because of its color, Mars has long been called the Red Planet. And when the Viking probes visited the planet in 1976, they found that the whole surface has a reddish-brown color.

A planet like Earth?

Mars is much like the Earth in several ways. It has ice caps at the poles, like the Earth. It rotates on its axis in a little over 24 hours, which means its day is about as long as the Earth's. Its axis is tilted in space (by 25°) like the Earth's, which means that it also has seasons.

▼ A sketch of Mars, based on a telescope observation of the planet. Vague markings can be seen on the surface, and the polar cap stands out.

◀ When the Viking probes visited Mars in 1976, they dropped landing craft onto the surface. The close-up pictures they took showed a landscape strewn with rocks.

IT'S AMAZING!

In 1931, Martians created a panic in America! The actor Orson Welles produced a realistic "It's happening now" type of radio drama based on H. G. Wells's classic science fiction book *The War of the Worlds*. In this book, invading Martians in terrifying war machines laid waste to the Earth.

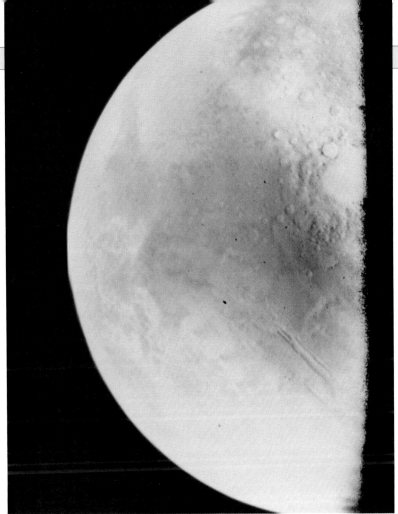

▶ A Viking probe took this picture as it approached Mars in 1976. It shows two of the planet's most prominent features, the Argyre Basin and Mariner Valley (see sketch below).

Q 1. The Argyre Basin is covered with frost. Elsewhere on Mars clouds can be seen above the mountains. What can we deduce from these observations?

Q 2. Mariner Valley is called the Martian Grand Canyon. It runs for 3,000 miles (5,000 km). If Arizona's Grand Canyon were as long, how far would it stretch across America?

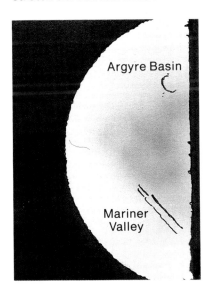

Argyre Basin

Mariner Valley

Life on Mars?

Because Mars appears to be like the Earth in some ways, people have long wondered whether there could be any life there. But visiting space probes have reported that conditions on Mars are far too harsh for life as we know it to survive.

Mars sometimes comes as close to the Earth as 35,000,000 miles (56,000,000 km). It is much smaller than the Earth, with a diameter of only 4,246 miles (6,794 km). It has only a trace of atmosphere, and not a breathable one; carbon dioxide is the main gas in the atmosphere. The climate on Mars is much colder than it is on Earth. During the day, the temperature scarcely rises above freezing, even on the equator. And at night the temperature can drop as low as $-330°F$ ($-200°C$).

Q 3. Mars is the only other planet in the Solar System on which human beings could land, explore and set up a colony. Why?

Jupiter

Jupiter lies more than three times as far away from the Sun as Mars, at a distance of some 483,000,000 miles (778,000,000 km). Yet at times it shines nearly as brightly as Mars. This is because it is a giant. Its diameter is 88,700 miles (142,800 km), more than 11 times that of the Earth.

Jupiter is not only much bigger than the Earth, it is also quite different in composition. It is made up almost entirely of hydrogen, not rock.

Through a telescope we can see more details on Jupiter than on any other planet. Its disc is crossed with light and dark reddish-brown bands. We call the light bands zones and the dark ones belts.

Space probes have shown that the bands are clouds in Jupiter's thick atmosphere, which have been drawn out parallel by the planet's swift rotation.

Q The clouds take about 10 hours to circle once around Jupiter. How fast do they move?

IT'S AMAZING!

Compared with the Earth, Jupiter is a giant, with 318 times more mass. But it is a midget compared with the Sun, which has 1,050 times Jupiter's mass.

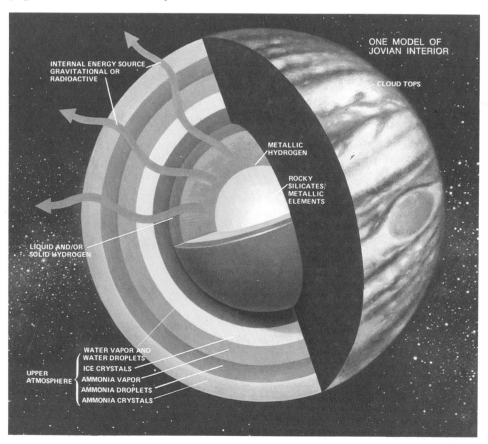

ONE MODEL OF JOVIAN INTERIOR

INTERNAL ENERGY SOURCE GRAVITATIONAL OR RADIOACTIVE

CLOUD TOPS

METALLIC HYDROGEN

ROCKY SILICATES/ METALLIC ELEMENTS

LIQUID AND/OR SOLID HYDROGEN

UPPER ATMOSPHERE
WATER VAPOR AND WATER DROPLETS
ICE CRYSTALS
AMMONIA VAPOR
AMMONIA DROPLETS
AMMONIA CRYSTALS

◀ Features of Jupiter. Beneath the colorful atmosphere are deep layers of liquid hydrogen and liquid metallic hydrogen above a rocky core. The other giant planets have much the same kind of structure.

▼ Planet Earth to scale.

46

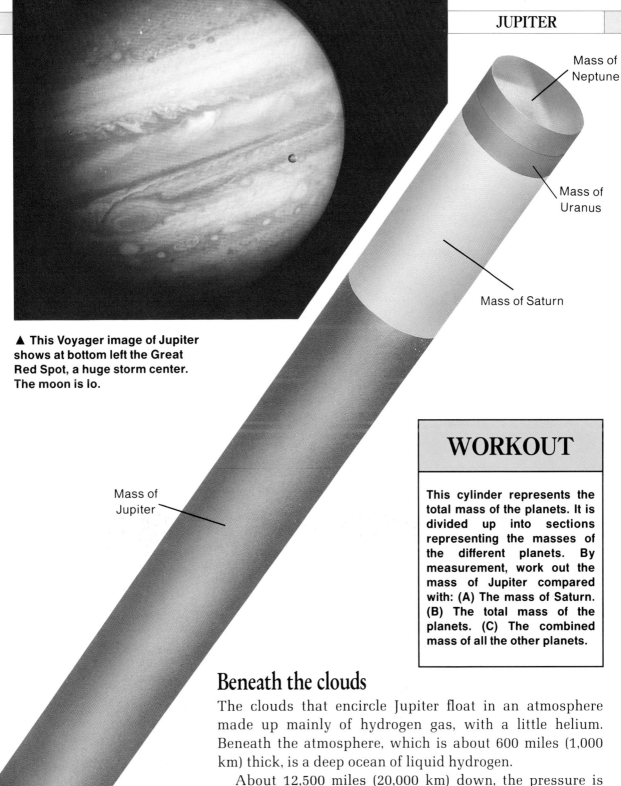

Mass of
Neptune

Mass of
Uranus

Mass of Saturn

▲ **This Voyager image of Jupiter shows at bottom left the Great Red Spot, a huge storm center. The moon is Io.**

Mass of
Jupiter

Combined mass of
Earth, Venus,
Mercury, Mars
and Pluto

WORKOUT

This cylinder represents the total mass of the planets. It is divided up into sections representing the masses of the different planets. By measurement, work out the mass of Jupiter compared with: (A) The mass of Saturn. (B) The total mass of the planets. (C) The combined mass of all the other planets.

Beneath the clouds

The clouds that encircle Jupiter float in an atmosphere made up mainly of hydrogen gas, with a little helium. Beneath the atmosphere, which is about 600 miles (1,000 km) thick, is a deep ocean of liquid hydrogen.

About 12,500 miles (20,000 km) down, the pressure is enormous and forces the hydrogen to become a kind of liquid metal. This liquid extends down to the center of the planet, where there is a core of rock about the same size as the Earth.

48

Saturn

With a diameter of 74,600 miles (120,000 km), Saturn is nearly as big as Jupiter. And it reflects sunlight brilliantly as well. But it appears much dimmer in the night sky. This is because it lies twice as far away from the Sun as Jupiter.

Saturn would appear even fainter were it not for its most outstanding feature, its beautiful system of rings. In a powerful telescope, they look magnificent. We can make out two bright rings (**A** and **B**), separated by a gap, and a faint inner one (**C**).

When the Voyager space probes visited Saturn, they discovered a number of other rings. They also found tiny moons orbiting close to the rings. As they whiz around, these moons help keep the ring particles in place, rather like a shepherd keeping a flock of sheep together. That is why they are called shepherd moons.

Q Saturn is a gas ball like Jupiter, but it is very much lighter. It has a relative density of only 0.7. What would happen if you could drop it into a huge bowl of water?

▼ If you could get very close to Saturn's rings and take a high-speed photograph, this might be the result. The picture would show lumps of rocks of different sizes, maybe covered with ice.

A ring

B ring

C ring

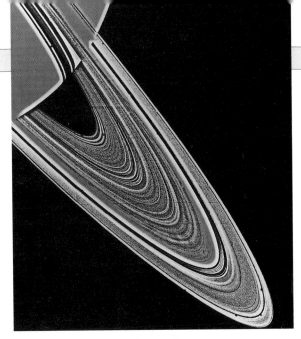

◄ A remarkable close-up picture of Saturn's rings taken by a Voyager probe. The rings prove to be made up of hundreds of separate ringlets.

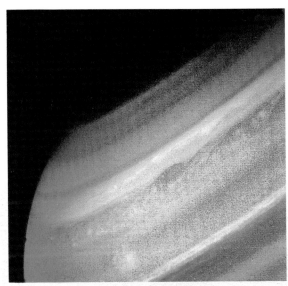

► Saturn's atmosphere is not as stormy as that of Jupiter. But violent activity can be seen in false-color Voyager pictures like this.

Match the pictures

Saturn's axis is tilted in relation to the plane of its orbit. From the Earth we therefore see different aspects of the rings at different times (see below).

Each aspect corresponds with a view we would see when Saturn is in one of the positions shown in the diagram on the right. Match each picture with a diagram.

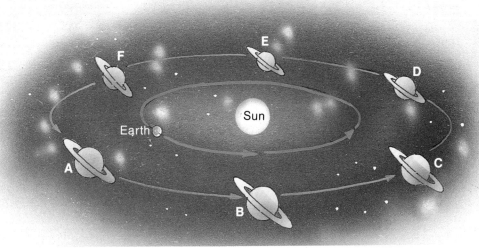

Far-distant worlds

Saturn, the sixth planet from the Sun, is the most distant one we can see with the naked eye. But powerful telescopes reveal three more planets at ever-increasing distances from the Sun.

The first is Uranus, which lies almost exactly twice as far away from the Sun as Saturn, at a distance of over 1,780,000,000 miles (2,860,000,000 km).

Q 1. Provide the name of the missing planet in this statement: The orbits of all the planets out to . . . . . would fit into the space between the orbits of Saturn and Uranus.

Twin Neptune

After Uranus comes the planet Neptune, nearly 2,800,000,000 miles (4,500,000,000 km) away from the Sun. In size, Neptune is a near-twin of Uranus, being only 4.5 percent smaller.

Q 2. The diameter of Uranus is 32,200 miles (51,800 km). What is Neptune's diameter (to three figures)?

Maverick Pluto

Pluto is so tiny and so far away – on average 3.6 billion miles (5.9 billion km), that it appears as a pinpoint of light even in the most powerful telescopes. It is usually even farther away than Neptune, but at the moment it isn't. This is because its peculiar orbit has taken it within Neptune's orbit. It will stay there until 1999. Then it will become the most distant planet again.

Pluto's orbit also takes it a long way above and below the orbits of the other planets.

▶ Like most of the other planets, Neptune spins on an axis that is slightly tilted at an angle (about 29°) in relation to the path it follows around the Sun. Uranus has a tilted axis, too. In fact, it is tilted right over at 98°, more than a right-angle! It therefore spins on its side as it circles the Sun.

Q 3. The Earth also has a tilted axis. How does this tilt affect us?

50

New planets

Until about 200 years ago people thought that there were only six planets because that was all they could see in the night sky.

But on the night of March 13, 1781, the English astronomer William Herschel spied what he took to be a comet in the constellation Gemini. But it wasn't a comet; it was a new planet, which came to be called Uranus.

Other astronomers began planet-hunting, but it was not until 1846 that another was found. It was called Neptune. More than 80 years went by before the third new planet, Pluto, was discovered in 1930.

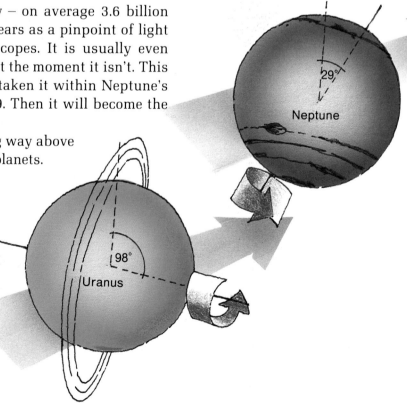

Neptune

Uranus

◄ This picture shows the planet Uranus as it might appear from a spaceship orbiting its moon Miranda. It is a montage of two images sent back by the Voyager 2 probe. Note the rings, which are too faint to be seen in telescopes.

▼ Neptune is deep blue in color because of methane gas in its atmosphere. White wisps of cloud and dark spots are dotted about. The dark spots are thought to be huge storm centers.

Many Moons

All the planets except Mercury and Venus have one or more moons circling around them. Altogether, there are over 60 moons in the Solar System. The Earth has just one, our nearest neighbor in space, which we call the Moon.

The Moon is the fifth largest moon. It is a ball of rock much like the Earth in composition. The moons of the other planets are quite different. Most of them are made up of a mixture of rock and ice. They also look quite different from our Moon. The most colorful one is Jupiter's moon Io, which is a vivid orange-yellow.

Titan, the biggest moon of Saturn, is unusual because it has a thick atmosphere. The gases in the atmosphere are nitrogen and methane. When it rains on Titan, it rains liquid methane!

Q 1. We use methane on Earth. What do we use it for?

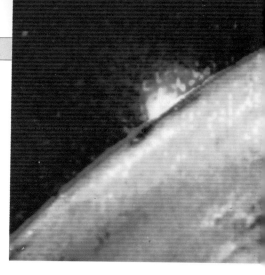

▲ Most moons in the Solar System are dead worlds, like our Moon. But Jupiter's moon Io is very much alive. Volcanoes pepper its colorful surface, spouting forth not rock, but molten sulfur!

Q 3. What color is sulfur?

Saturn is like a miniature solar system, with at least 22 moons circling around it. Those shown in the diagram are the ones we can see in telescopes.

Q 2. The other 12 tiny moons were discovered by which space probes?

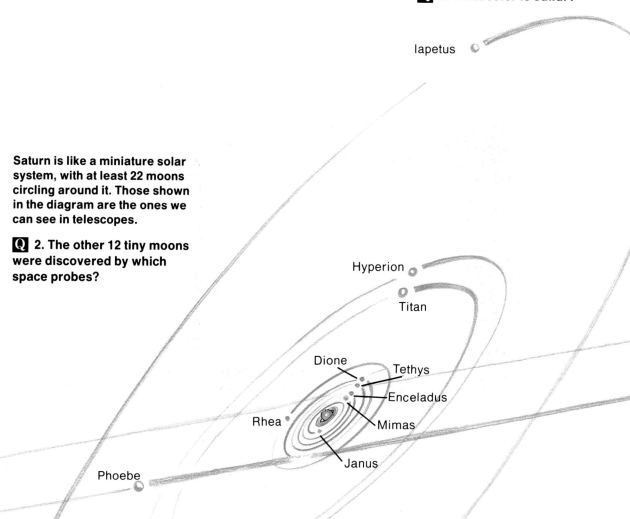

Iapetus

Hyperion

Titan

Dione

Tethys

Enceladus

Rhea

Mimas

Janus

Phoebe

52

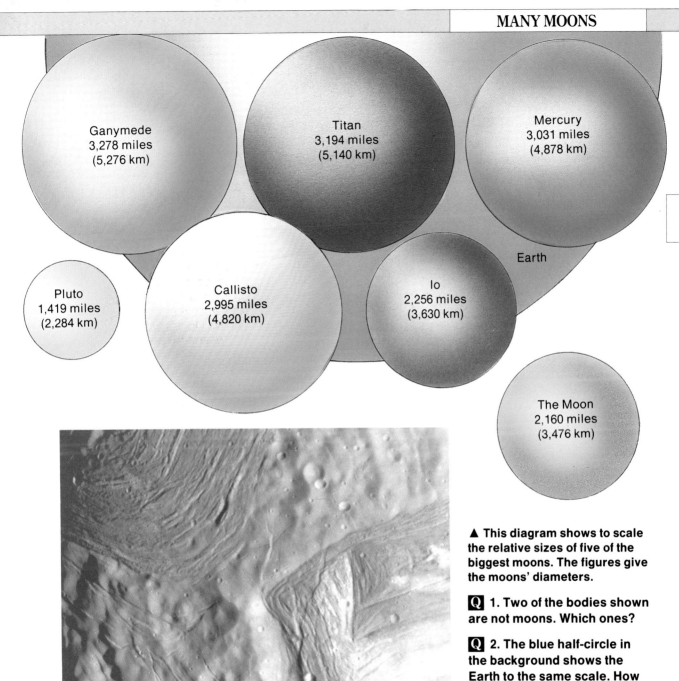

Ganymede
3,278 miles
(5,276 km)

Titan
3,194 miles
(5,140 km)

Mercury
3,031 miles
(4,878 km)

Earth

Pluto
1,419 miles
(2,284 km)

Callisto
2,995 miles
(4,820 km)

Io
2,256 miles
(3,630 km)

The Moon
2,160 miles
(3,476 km)

▲ This diagram shows to scale the relative sizes of five of the biggest moons. The figures give the moons' diameters.

Q 1. Two of the bodies shown are not moons. Which ones?

Q 2. The blue half-circle in the background shows the Earth to the same scale. How many Ganymedes could you put in a globe the size of the Earth?

All smashed up

Miranda, one of Uranus's moons, has the most curious surface of any moon. It is a patchwork of quite different landscapes butted together. Astronomers think that long ago the moon may have been smashed to pieces when it hit an asteroid. Then the pieces came together again under gravity to create the fantastic landscape we see today.

Probing the Solar System

For centuries astronomers had to observe the planets from afar. But nowadays they can observe them close-up using space probes. These spacecraft make long journeys into the depths of space over periods of time measured in years and over distances measured in millions and billions of miles.

54

Beginning in 1962, probes have visited and reported back from all the planets except Pluto. They have carried all kinds of instruments, which have revealed many of the secrets of the planets and their moons. Most importantly, they have carried cameras, which have sent back the most amazing photographs.

Escaping from the Earth

Before a probe can begin its journey to a distant planet, it has to escape from the powerful pull of Earth's gravity. To do this, it must be propelled from the Earth at a colossal speed, 25,000 mph (40,000 km/h)! This speed is called the Earth's escape velocity.

Q **1.** Flying in a jumbo jet, it takes you about 6 hours to cover the 3,000 miles (5,000 km) from New York to London. How long would the journey take if you could hitch a ride on an escaping space probe?

▲ The Voyager probes each carry a disc on which are recorded typical "Sounds of Earth," along with messages from world leaders. One day, many thousands of years in the future, intelligent beings elsewhere in the Universe might find them.

Q **2. What would your message be to extraterrestrials?**

◄ The Galileo probe was launched from the space shuttle in 1989. It began a roundabout journey to Jupiter, which took it twice past Earth and once past Venus. Each time it passed them, it used their gravity to increase its speed.

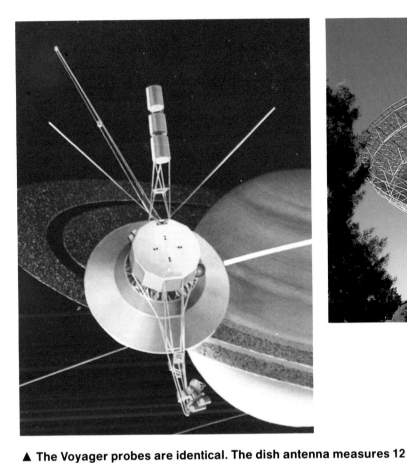

▲ The Parkes radio telescope in Australia, used to receive signals from Voyager 2 when it flew past Neptune in August 1989.

Q 2. At that time, Neptune was 2,700,000,000 miles (4,400,000,000 km) from the Earth. How long did it take Voyager's radio signals to reach Earth? (Radio waves travel at the speed of light, 186,000 miles or 300,000 km a second.)

▲ The Voyager probes are identical. The dish antenna measures 12 feet (3.7 meters) across. The electricity to power the instruments, cameras and radio comes from a nuclear battery, called a radioisotope thermoelectric generator.

Q 1. Why couldn't solar cells, which change sunlight into electricity, be used to provide power?

Boosting speed

After a probe reaches escape velocity, its launch rocket separates and the probe coasts, without power, the rest of the way to its target planet. As it fights against Earth's gravity, it gradually slows down to a speed of a few thousand miles an hour. But as it draws near to its target planet, it is pulled by the planet's gravity and speeds up again.

Some probes use the pull of one planet not only to increase their speed, but also to change their direction so that they can visit another planet. Voyager 2 carried out this "sling-shot" – or gravity-assist – maneuver three times on its record-breaking mission to Neptune.

Milestones

ABOUT 3000 BC Sumerian and Babylonian stargazers in the Middle East began recording their observations of the stars and planets.

ABOUT 2000 BC Ancient Britons built Stonehenge, near Salisbury, probably the first astronomical observatory.

ABOUT 1500 BC Ancient Americans built "America's Stonehenge," near Salisbury, New Hampshire, also of astronomical importance.

ABOUT 330 BC Aristotle and other Greek philosophers considered the Earth to be the center of the Universe, with the Sun, the Moon and the stars circling around it.

ABOUT 300 BC One Greek philosopher, named Aristarchus, disagreed with Aristotle's viewpoint. He figured that the Earth and the planets all circled around the Sun.

ABOUT AD 150 Ptolemy, a Greek from Alexandria, compiled an encyclopedia detailing the astronomical knowledge of the ancients, in particular the Earth-centered view of the Universe.

1543 The Polish priest/astronomer, Nicolaus Copernicus, overturned the established view of the Universe by suggesting that the Earth and the planets circle around the Sun.

1576 The Danish astronomer Tycho Brahe began meticulous observations of the movements of the planets.

1609 Brahe's successor, the German Johannes Kepler, showed that the planets move around the Sun in elliptical orbits.

1609/10 The Italian scientist Galileo built one of the first successful telescopes and trained it on the heavens. He became the first to see the mountains of the Moon and the phases of Venus.

1705 The English Astronomer Royal, Edmond Halley, predicted the return in 1758 of the comet now named after him.

1781 On the night of Tuesday, March 13, the German-born English astronomer William Herschel discovered Uranus, the first new planet since ancient times.

1801 The Italian astronomer Giuseppe Piazzi discovered the first and largest asteroid, Ceres.

1846 On September 23, the German astronomer Johann Gottfried Galle discovered another new planet, Neptune.

1930 The American astronomer Clyde Tombaugh discovered a third new planet on February 18 at Lowell Observatory in Flagstaff, Arizona.

1958 The first U.S. satellite, Explorer 1, made the first scientific discovery of the Space Age – the Van Allen belts of radiation around the Earth.

1962 The U.S. probe Mariner 2 made the first successful flyby of another planet, Venus.

1969-1972 U.S. Apollo astronauts landed on the Moon and explored the surface on foot.

1974 Pioneer 10 became the first probe to reach the giant planet Jupiter.

1979-1989 The Voyager 2 probe visited four planets, Jupiter, Saturn, Uranus and Neptune, before leaving the Solar System.

1992 A mini-planet was discovered beyond the orbit of Pluto, perhaps one of many in the distant reaches of the Solar System.

Glossary

ASTEROIDS Small rocky bodies that circle the Sun, mainly in a "belt" between the orbits of Mars and Jupiter. They are also called the minor planets.

ASTROLOGY Study of the positions of the heavenly bodies with a view to foretelling future events in people's lives.

ASTRONOMY The scientific study of the heavens and the bodies therein: the Sun, the Moon, the planets, their moons, the stars and the galaxies.

ATMOSPHERE The layer of gases around the Earth or another heavenly body.

AURORA A colorful glow seen in far northern and far southern skies, produced when charged particles from the Sun collide with particles in the upper atmosphere. See also **NORTHERN LIGHTS; SOUTHERN LIGHTS.**

CHROMOSPHERE The lower layer of the Sun's atmosphere, which is pink in color. We can see it during a total eclipse of the Sun.

COMET A "dirty snowball" of rock, ice and dust, which starts to shine when it approaches the Sun.

CONSTELLATIONS Imaginary patterns the bright stars make in the heavens.

CORONA A white halo, or "crown" we can see around the Sun during a total solar eclipse. It is the Sun's outer atmosphere.

COSMIC RAYS Radiation that comes from outer space.

CRATERS Holes on the surface of a planet or a moon, made by falling meteorites or by erupting volcanoes.

ECLIPSE The passing of one heavenly body in front of another, blotting out its light. We see a solar eclipse, or an eclipse of the Sun, when the Moon passes in front of the Sun. We see a lunar eclipse, or an eclipse of the Moon, when the Moon moves into the Earth's shadow.

ELLIPTICAL ORBIT An orbit that has an elliptical, or oval, shape. The planets travel in elliptical orbits around the Sun. Moons travel in elliptical orbits around their planets.

EQUINOXES Times of the year when the lengths of the day and the night are equal all over the world. This happens twice: on March 21 (the vernal, or spring, equinox); and on September 23 (the autumnal equinox).

EVENING STAR Usually the planet Venus when we see it shining brightly in the western sky at sunset.

GALAXY An "island" of stars in space. Galaxies are usually elliptical or spiral in shape. The spiral galaxy to which our Sun belongs is known as the Milky Way.

GRAVITY The force with which the Earth attracts any object near it. The other heavenly bodies exert a similar force. Gravity is one of the great forces of the Universe; it literally holds the Universe together.

HEAVENLY BODY A body we see in the heavens, or the night sky, such as the Moon, a planet or a star.

HYDROGEN The simplest of all the chemical elements and also the most plentiful element in the Universe.

INTERPLANETARY Between the planets.

LUNAR Relating to the Moon.

57

58

MARE A large plain on the Moon. *Mare* (plural *maria*) is the Latin word for "sea." Early astronomers thought that the maria, or dark areas we see on the Moon, could be water-filled seas.

METEOR A streak of light we see in the night sky. Meteors occur when bits of rock from outer space plunge through the atmosphere and burn up.

METEORITE A piece of rock from outer space big enough to survive its passage through the atmosphere and reach the ground.

MORNING STAR The planet Venus when it shines brightly in the eastern sky at dawn.

NORTHERN LIGHTS The display of aurora in the Northern Hemisphere; the aurora borealis. See also **SOUTHERN LIGHTS.**

NUCLEAR FUSION The process by which the Sun produces its energy. It is a process in which the nuclei (centers) of hydrogen atoms combine together. When this happens, enormous energy is given out as light, heat and other radiation.

ORBIT The path in space of one body around another, such the Earth around the Sun and the Moon around the Earth.

PHASES The different shapes of the Moon we see in the sky during the month, as more or less of its surface is lit up by the Sun. Venus shows noticeable phases as well.

PLANETS Large bodies that circle in space around the Sun. The Earth is a planet. There are eight others, some much smaller, and some much bigger than the Earth. Other stars probably have planets circling around them.

PROBE A spacecraft sent far into space to explore other heavenly bodies, such as the Moon, the planets and comets.

PROMINENCE A fountain of gas that shoots high above the surface of the Sun. We can see prominences only during a total eclipse of the Sun.

RADIATION Rays, given off by the Sun and the stars: for example, light rays, X-rays, ultraviolet rays, infrared rays and radio waves. These are all different kinds of electromagnetic radiation.

SATELLITE A small body that circles around a larger one in space; a moon. Most of the planets have natural satellites. The Earth has one, the Moon. Saturn has more than 20. Earth also now has thousands of artificial satellites circling around it, launched into orbit by space scientists.

SEASONS Periods of the year marked by noticeable changes in the weather, particularly in temperature. Many parts of the world experience four distinct seasons: spring, summer, autumn and winter. Seasonal changes also take place on other planets, especially Mars. See also **EQUINOXES; SOLSTICES.**

SHEPHERD MOONS Tiny moons found near the rings of Saturn and other planets. Somehow they help keep the ring particles in place.

SOLAR SYSTEM The family of the Sun, which travels through space as a unit. It has the Sun at its center, and around the Sun circle nine planets (including the Earth), the "belt" of asteroids, and many comets.

SOLAR WIND A stream of charged particles given off by the Sun.

SOLSTICES Times of the year when the Sun reaches its highest and lowest points in the sky at noon. In the Northern Hemisphere, it reaches its highest point on about June 21 (summer solstice), and its lowest on December 21 (winter solstice). The dates are reversed in the Southern Hemisphere.

SOUTHERN LIGHTS The display of aurora that occurs in the Southern Hemisphere; the aurora australis.

STAR A gaseous body that produces its own energy by nuclear fusion. It releases this energy as light, heat and other radiation. The Sun is our local star.

SUN Our local star, whose enormous gravity holds the Solar System together over distances of billions of miles.

SUNSPOT An area on the Sun's surface that is darker and cooler than normal. Sunspots come and go regularly over a period of about 11 years.

TERMINATOR The boundary between the sunlit and dark halves of the Moon or a planet.

TERRESTRIAL Relating to the Earth.

TIDES The rise and fall of the oceans, which occur twice a day. They occur because of the pull of the Moon's gravity.

TOTAL ECLIPSE An eclipse of the Sun in which the disc of the Moon completely covers the disc of the Sun.

UNIVERSE Everything that exists: the Earth, the Moon, the Sun, the planets, the stars and even space itself.

ZODIAC An imaginary band in the heavens in which the Sun, Moon and planets are always found. It is occupied by 12 constellations, the constellations of the zodiac.

For Further Reading

Alter, Anna.
Destination: Outer space.
Childrens Press, Chicago, 1988.

Asimov, Issac.
Our Solar System.
Gareth Stevens, Milwaukee, 1988.

Brewer, Duncan.
Planet Guides: Mercury and the Sun.
Marshall Cavendish, New York, 1993.

Brown, Peter.
Astronomy.
Facts on File, New York, 1984

Fradin, Dennis.
Astronomy.
Childrens Press, Chicago, 1987.

Lambert, David.
The Solar System.
Franklin Watts, New York, 1984.

59

Answers

Page 9
1. The nearest stars are about 24 billion miles (39 billion km) away.
☆ **Hint:** Calculate the number of minutes in 4 years; divide by 8, then multiply by the Sun-Earth distance.

Page 10
A point travels at 1,037 mph (1,669 km).
☆ **Hint:** The circumference of the Earth is $\pi \times$ diameter. A point travels this distance in 24 hours.

Page 11
1. The Earth travels about 584,040,000 miles (940,000,000 km) in its orbit each year.
☆**Hint:** The Earth travels a distance of $2\pi \times r$ in its orbit.
2. We correct the calendar by including a leap year of 366 days every fourth year; the extra day is February 29th.

Page 13
1. The seasons are reversed because when one hemisphere is tilted toward the Sun, the other is tilted away.
2. The pictures and dates are as follows:
A - Mar. 21 or Sept. 23; **B** - Dec. 21;
C - June 21; **D** - Sept. 23 or Mar. 21

Page 16
1. The lunar calendar year of 12 lunar months is 11 days less than the ordinary, or solar calendar year. 12 lunar months is $12 \times 29\frac{1}{2}$ days.
Match the phases
First Quarter - **Z**; Full Moon - **M**;
Last Quarter - **A**; New Moon - **H**.

Investigate
As you turn, you always face the ball. The Moon moves in a similar way, with the same side always facing the Earth. We say the Moon has a captured rotation.

Page 17
We get another high tide when the Moon is on the opposite side of the Earth and exerts the least gravitational force on the ocean.

Page 18
1. Any water on the Moon's surface would soon evaporate into space.
2. The Earth's atmosphere helped protect it from the bombardment. Also, any craters that did form long, long ago have been worn away because of the action of water, wind and other elements.

Page 19
1. The highlands are the oldest regions of the Moon; they are covered with craters. The seas are much younger, because they have fewer craters.
2. Through binoculars, the Moon appears the right-side up; through an astronomical telescope, it appears upside-down.

Page 20
1. The change in weight came about because objects on the Moon weigh only one-sixth what they do on Earth, because the Moon's gravity is only one-sixth that of Earth. But their mass remains the same.
2. The Apollo astronauts had to wear spacesuits to give them oxygen to breathe. The suits also helped protect them from the cold temperatures of space and from the heat and other harmful radiation given out by the Sun.

Page 21
1. Car engines need to take in air to burn the gasoline. The Moon has no air.
2. Armalcolite was named after the first

three Apollo astronauts: Arm(strong), Al(drin), and Co(llins).

Page 22
1. A lunar eclipse takes longer because the Earth casts a much bigger shadow than the Moon.
2. A solar eclipse occurs at a New Moon.
Workout
The Sun is about 400 times bigger than the Moon, and is about 400 times farther away. This means that the Sun appears about the same size as the Moon in the sky.

Page 23
A lunar eclipse occurs at a Full Moon.
Workout
The Moon spends 1 hour 34 minutes in total eclipse.
☆ **Hint:** Remember that the edge of the Moon that enters the Earth's shadow travels one diameter before the Moon is in total eclipse.

Page 27
Investigate
The distances of the planets from the Sun in AUs (to 2 significant figures) are: Mercury, 0.39; Venus, 0.72; Mars, 1.5; Jupiter, 5.2; Saturn, 9.5; Uranus, 19; Neptune, 30; Pluto, 39.

Page 29
Workout
The relative density of Jupiter is 1.33. This low density fits in with Jupiter being made mainly of gaseous materials.
☆ **Hint:** Mass = volume × density. If Jupiter had the same density as the Earth, it would have 1,316 times the Earth's mass. But it has only 318 times the Earth's mass. Therefore it must have only $318 \div 1,316$ times the density.

Page 30
Investigate
Mars and Jupiter are the best planets to

choose because they are bright and appear in a dark sky; Venus is bright but usually appears in a light sky because it stays near the Sun.

Page 32
1. The Orion nebula is in the constellation Orion. The nebula is special because it can easily be seen with the naked eye.
2. Many galaxies have the same shape.

Page 33
The lumps came together because of their gravity.

Page 34
The "open" orbit of the comet is totally different from the "closed" orbits of the planets. The comet's tail always points away from the Sun.

Page 35
1. The comet was moving against the background of stars. Therefore the stars left trails as the camera moved to follow the comet.
2. With no sunlight, plants could not grow. Soon there was no food for the dinosaurs to eat and they starved to death.

Page 37
Workout
About 860 million tons (770 million tonnes) of rock were gouged out.
☆ **Hint:** First find the area of cross-section; multiply this by the thickness to get the volume; then multiply the volume by the density.

Page 40
1. B and **D**.
2. Venus is a morning star, Mercury an evening star.

Page 41
Mercury looks somewhat like the Moon.

Page 42
Almost all living things must breathe the

oxygen in the air or dissolved in water; the bodies of most living things contain water, which is used to circulate vital materials to and from the body's cells.

Page 43
1. The diameter of the Earth's inner core is 1,990 miles (3,200 km).
2. Oxygen is essential for life.

Page 45
1. There is water in Mars's atmosphere.
2. The Martian Grand Canyon would stretch from Los Angeles to Boston.
3. Mars is the only planet with a reasonable temperature and a solid surface.

Page 46
The clouds move at a speed of about 27,850 mph (44,830 km/h).
☆ **Hint:** They travel one circumference of the planet every 10 hours.

Page 47
Workout
Jupiter has (**A**) 3.3 times Saturn's mass; (**B**) 0.7 the total mass of all the planets; (**C**) 2.5 times the combined mass of all the other planets.

Page 48
Saturn would float in water!

Page 49
Match the pictures
A6, B2, C5, D1, E4, F3.

Page 50
1. Mars.
2. The diameter of Neptune is about 30,800 miles (49,500 km).
3. The tilt of the Earth's axis brings about the seasons.

Page 52
1. Methane is used for cooking and heating; it is the main component in natural gas.
2. The Voyager probes discovered Saturn's other moons.

3. Sulfur is yellow.

Page 53
1. Mercury and Pluto are not moons; they are the two smallest planets.
2. 14 Ganymedes would fit into an Earth globe.
☆ **Hint:** The volume of the Earth is proportional to its radius (**RE**) cubed; the volume of Ganymede is proportional to its radius (**RG**) cubed. So the Earth has (**RE ÷ RG**) cubed Ganymede's volume.

Page 54
You would cross the Atlantic in 7 mins 12 secs.

Page 55
1. Solar cells couldn't be used because sunlight is too weak in the outer part of the Solar System.
2. The signals from Voyager at Neptune took over 4 hours to reach Earth.

Index

64

Picture Credits

Most pictures were supplied by NASA through Spacecharts Photo Library, to whom many thanks are due.

Thanks are also due to the following for providing the remainder of the pictures.

European Space Agency: 35B
Graham Beehag Books: Title page, 6, 8, 15, 18, 20, 21, 32, 38, 46, 47, 51, 52, 53, 54,
Robin Kerrod: 13, 23, 37, 42, 55
Spacecharts: 32
Kitt Peak National Observatory: 35T